FAR-OUT GUIDE
to the
SOLAR SYSTEM

FAR-OUT GUIDE TO
MERCURY

Mary Kay Carson

Bailey Books
an imprint of
Enslow Publishers, Inc.
40 Industrial Road
Box 398
Berkeley Heights, NJ 07922
USA
http://www.enslow.com

For Stella Joy Thomas, who's as swift a runner as Mercury

Bailey Books, an imprint of Enslow Publishers, Inc.

Library of Congress Cataloging-in-Publication Data

Carson, Mary Kay.
      Far-out guide to Mercury / Mary Kay Carson.
          p. cm. — (Far-out guide to the solar system)
      Summary: "Presents information about Mercury, including fast facts, history,
and technology used to study the planet"—Provided by publisher.
      Includes bibliographical references and index.
      ISBN 978-0-7660-3180-7 (Library Ed.)
      ISBN 978-1-59845-181-8 (Paperback Ed.)
      1. Mercury (Planet)—Juvenile literature. 2. Solar system—Juvenile literature. I. Title.
      QB611.C37 2011
      523.41—dc22

                        2009006486

Printed in China

052010 Leo Paper Group, Heshan City, Guangdong, China

10 9 8 7 6 5 4 3 2 1

Image Credits: ESA, p. 42; ESA – Image by C. Carreau, p. 40; ESA – Image by AOES Medialab, pp. 38–39; Lunar and Planetary Institute, p. 17; NASA, p. 13; NASA Goddard Space Flight Center, p. 18; NASA/Johns Hopkins University Applied Physics Laboratory/Carnegie Institution of Washington, pp. 1, 9, 26, 28, 30, 32, 34, 35, 36, 37; NASA/JPL, pp. 4–5; NASA/JPL/USGS, pp. 3, 15; NASA/Mariner 10, Astrogeology Team, U.S. Geological Survey, p. 20; NASA/Michael Carroll/Alien Volcanoes by Lopes and Carroll, The Johns Hopkins University Press, 2008., pp. 6, 24–25; National Radio Astronomy Observatory/Associated Universities, Inc./National Science Foundation, p. 12; Tom Uhlman Photography, p. 10.

Cover Image: NASA/Johns Hopkins University Applied Physics Laboratory/Carnegie Institution of Washington
The cover illustration shows the Messenger *spacecraft arriving at Mercury in 2008.*

CONTENTS

Mercury

MERCURY is the planet nearest the Sun. (Note that the planets' distances are not shown to scale.) Mars, Earth, Venus, and Mercury are the solar system's land-covered, or terrestrial, planets. Mercury is the least well-known of these four rocky worlds.

INTRODUCTION

Sunrise on Mercury can be quite a show. The Sun comes over the horizon and grows larger as it rises. Once high in the black sky, the Sun pauses and then moves backward along its path a bit. The odd sunrise is a long show, too. Nearly six months of Earth time pass between one sunrise and the next on Mercury! You will learn lots more far-out facts about Mercury in this book. Just keep reading!

EXTREME PLANET

Mercury is a planet of extremes. It is the smallest in the solar system. Mercury is the fastest planet, too. It travels through space at the highest speed. Mercury is also the planet nearest the Sun. Temperatures there

NO person or spacecraft has ever landed on Mercury. This illustration shows what Mercury's surface might be like. The Sun looks nearly three times as big from Mercury as it does from Earth.

get extremely hot, but also extremely cold. Its surface is one of the oldest in the solar system. Mercury is the planet with the least atmosphere. It is practically airless! Mercury is also one of the least-explored planets. Dozens of spacecraft have gone to both Venus and Mars. But only two robotic spacecraft have ever visited Mercury. Why do you think this is so?

Mercury is dangerously close to the Sun. The Sun's powerful heat and rays damage most spacecraft. So little exploration means Mercury still has many mysteries. Scientists have many questions about the planet: Why is Mercury so dense? What lies at its center? Did volcanoes shape the planet? One robotic spacecraft is braving the heat to find some answers. It is sending back the first views of all of Mercury. The space probe will also search for something almost unbelievable. It will look for ice on the planet closest to the Sun.

FAR-OUT FACT

LONG DAYS, SHORT YEARS

Mercury speeds around the Sun at 47,873 meters (157,062 feet) per *second*. It only takes 88 Earth days for Mercury to orbit the Sun. Four years would pass on Mercury between your Earth birthdays. While Mercury's year is short, its day drags on and on. It takes Mercury more than 1,407 hours to spin around once, which is one day. That means that one Mercury day lasts nearly two months of Earth time!

CHAPTER I

MYSTERIOUS MERCURY

Seeing Mercury from Earth can be tough. It only appears in the night sky right before sunrise or just after sunset. Mercury's closeness to the Sun makes it hard to see with telescopes, too. Having to look toward the Sun when observing Mercury is like trying to see a flickering candle next to a roaring campfire.

Radar gets around this problem. A radar telescope can send radar beams toward Mercury at any time of day. Radar is not blinded by sunlight. Radar has helped scientists discover many things about Mercury. They were finally able to measure how long a day lasts on Mercury using radar in 1965. Radar telescopes helped make another surprising discovery about Mercury in 1991.

is an airless, lifeless world covered in craters.

RADAR TELESCOPES

A radar telescope is not a tube you look through, like a backyard telescope. Instead, it looks like a big satellite dish. Radar telescopes send out pulses of radio waves toward a planet or other object in space. The waves hit the object and their echoes bounce back to Earth. The time between pulses and bounces—and how the radio waves change— is used to make maps and pictures of planets, asteroids, moons, and even the rings of Saturn.

THESE antennae are part of the Very Large Array (VLA). The VLA is an observatory in New Mexico. It studies planets and stars with radar and radio signals. It was part of the radar system that studied Mercury's ice in 1991.

IMPROBABLE ICE

Scientist Duane Muhleman uses radar telescopes to study planets. He has studied Mars, Venus, and Saturn. In 1991, Muhleman was bouncing radar beams off Mercury. He was making a map of its surface. At the time, more than half of Mercury had never been seen before.

Muhleman's team sent powerful radar beams toward the planet. Radar telescopes received the echoes that bounced off the planet. A computer turned the radar information into the map on page 12. One part of the radar map shocked scientists. There was a bright circle at the top of Mercury. The radar beam had hit and bounced off something very shiny at Mercury's north pole. That "shiny something" was too bright to be rock. "The only other places we've seen [the radar] do this are at the ice caps on Mars," Muhleman told reporters.

Muhleman and his team had a hard time believing what they were seeing at first. "The general reaction was . . . 'that can't be ice, can it?'" Muhleman said. "But once you think about it . . . it makes perfect sense." How can hot Mercury have ice? The planet is close to the Sun.

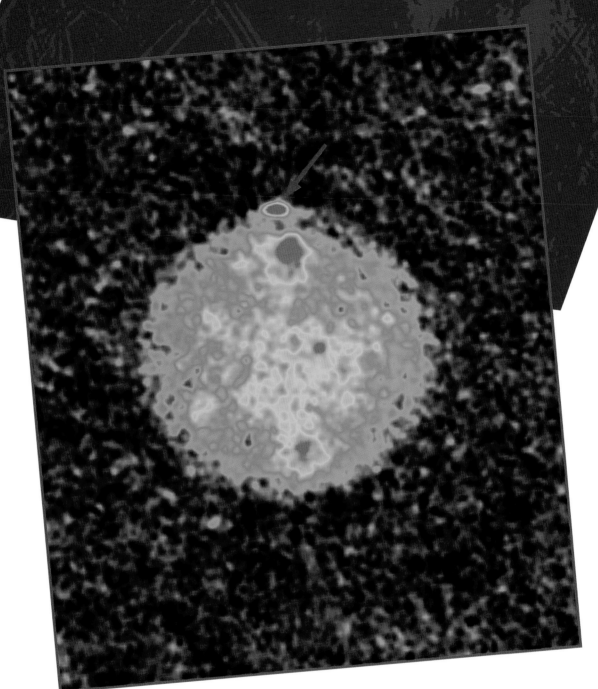

THIS is the radar map of Mercury that Duane Muhleman and his team created. The red areas on the map are where the most echoes bounced back. The arrow points to the small red circle on top that is the "shiny something" thought to be ice.

But some parts of Mercury are always dark and cold—cold enough to keep water frozen solid.

AIRLESS AND CRATERED

Mercury might remind you of Earth's Moon. They are similar in size. Both are lifeless, silent, gray worlds. Each is covered in craters and dusty hills. Mercury and the Moon have black star-filled skies, even during the day.

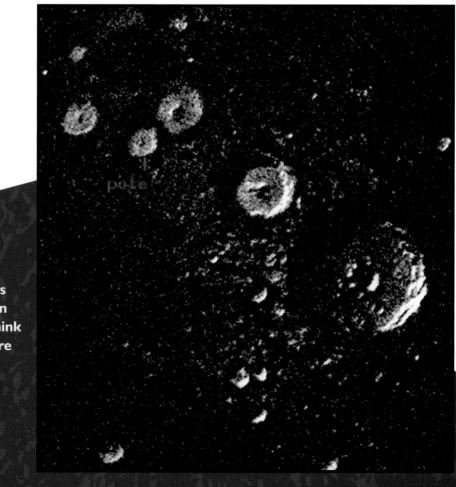

THIS is a radar image of Mercury's north pole taken in 1999. Scientists think the bright areas are ice on dark crater floors.

These two worlds are similar for a reason. Neither has an atmosphere. No blanket of air surrounds the Moon or Mercury. Sounds cannot travel without air. Skies cannot be blue, red, or any other color without an atmosphere to scatter sunlight.

Air also holds in heat. Mercury is closest to the Sun. But Venus is hotter because of its smothering thick atmosphere. The sunlit side of Mercury is cooked by solar rays eleven times more powerful than here on Earth. Meanwhile, the dark side of Mercury is deep-freeze cold.

FAR-OUT FACT

MARINER'S HALF OF MERCURY

Mariner 10 was the first spacecraft to visit Mercury. The robotic space probe made three passes by the planet in 1974 and 1975. Each time *Mariner 10* flew past, the same side of Mercury was lit up by the Sun. So only one half of Mercury was photographed by the spacecraft. The other half of Mercury was not photographed up close until 34 years later when the space probe *MESSENGER* flew by.

THIS *Mariner 10* image shows some of Mercury's many craters.

Temperatures on airless Mercury vary more than on any other planet. Days can be 600° Celsius (1,100° Fahrenheit) hotter than nights! Temperatures go from tin-melting hot to as cold as Saturn, a planet nearly twenty-five times farther from the Sun.

Mercury's lack of air is part of the reason craters cover it. Atmospheres usually shield planets and moons from incoming space rocks. Smaller asteroids, meteoroids, and comets slow down and burn up as they pass through air. But Mercury does not have air to stop these incoming objects. Mercury's craters also last longer than craters on planets with air, wind, and rain. Weather and a shifting surface erase craters on Earth. Mercury has kept its ancient craters for billions of years. Mercury's little-changing surface is the oldest of any planet in the solar system.

DARK, DEEP, AND ICY

Mercury's craters come in all sizes. The deep ones have steep walls. These cast shadows on the floors of the craters. Many of the crater floors at Mercury's north and south poles are always dark. Sunlight never touches them,

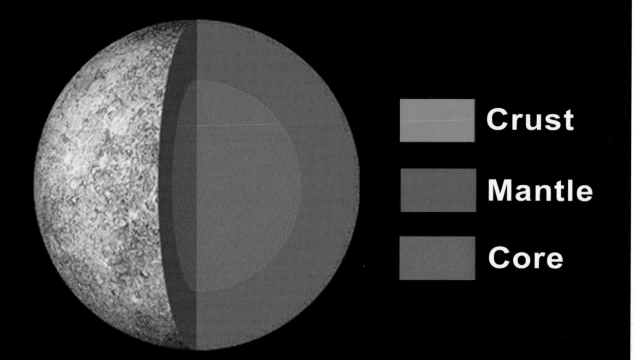

MERCURY

Crust

Mantle

Core

LEFTOVER CORE

Mercury is only a bit bigger than the Moon. But it is four and a half times as heavy. Its large mass and compact size make it the densest planet in the solar system. Mercury has a giant iron core. Its core makes up nearly three-quarters of Mercury's diameter. Why is Mercury mostly core? Scientists think that something the size of a planet might have slammed into Mercury long ago. The crash blasted off much of Mercury's outer layers, leaving mostly core.

CUTTING IN FRONT OF THE SUN

When Mercury passes between the Sun and Earth, Mercury is seen from Earth as a small black dot moving across the Sun. When an object in space passes in front of a larger object, it is called a transit. Early astronomers used transits to study Mercury. They used its silhouetted form to estimate Mercury's size and looked for signs of an atmosphere. Transits of Mercury are rare. The last ones happened in 2003 and 2006. The next will be in 2016.

THIS is an image of the 2003 transit of Mercury.

so they never warm up. Where it is dark on Mercury, it is very cold. And where it is always dark, it stays very cold.

Is there ice in Mercury's dark craters? Duane Muhleman's radar map shows that there is. Since that 1991 discovery, other radar telescopes have also observed ice at Mercury's poles. How did this ice get there? There is no water naturally on Mercury. Scientists think that comets and asteroids could have delivered ice to the planet. Once the ice was in the dark, cold craters, it could have stayed there for millions of years. Will we ever know if the shiny something at Mercury's poles is definitely ice? The spacecraft *MESSENGER* aims to find out.

Mercury at a Glance

Diameter: 4,879 kilometers (3,032 miles)

Volume: 5.4% of Earth's

Mass: 5.5% of Earth's, or 330,220,000,000 trillion kilograms

Gravity: A 75-pound kid would weigh 28½ pounds

Position: First planet from the Sun

Average Distance from Sun: 57,909,175 kilometers (35,983,095 miles)

Day Length (One Spin): 1,407½ hours

Year Length: 88 Earth days

Color: Gray

Atmosphere: None

Surface: Rock

Minimum/Maximum Surface Temperature: −173/427° Celsius (−279/801° Fahrenheit)

Moons: None

Rings: None

Namesake: Messenger of the Roman gods

Symbol:

Planet Fast Facts

★ Mercury is the smallest and fastest
  planet in the solar system, and nearest
  to the Sun.

★ Mercury orbits at 172,341 kilometers (107,088 miles)
  per hour! That is more than 1½ times faster than Earth's
  speed of 107,229 kilometers (66,629 miles) per hour.

★ Temperatures on Mercury swing between extremely hot
  and extremely cold. They vary more than any other planet
  in the solar system.

★ Days on Mercury can be 600° Celsius (1,100° Fahrenheit)
  hotter than nights!

★ When lit by the Sun, Mercury's surface can reach
  temperatures hot enough to melt lead and tin.

★ Mercury is closer to the Sun than Venus. But Venus
  gets hotter because of its thick atmosphere.

★ The Sun's rays are eleven times stronger on Mercury
  than on Earth. The Sun also looks nearly three times
  as big from Mercury as it does from Earth.

★ Mercury spins around with no tilt, so it has no seasons.

★ Mercury has no air and no significant atmosphere.
  This means, like on Earth's moon, the sky is always black.
  Stars are out even during the day.

★ A thin layer of atoms—called an exosphere—surrounds
  Mercury. Its exosphere includes sodium, water vapor,
  helium, and hydrogen.

★ Much of Mercury's surface has not changed in billions
  of years. Its surface is the oldest of any planet in the
  solar system.

★ Craters, cliffs, and volcanoes cover Mercury's ancient, dusty, gray surface.

★ Mercury's melted iron center, or core, is giant. That gives the small world lots of mass. Mercury is the densest planet in the solar system.

★ Some of Mercury's deep craters at its north and south poles are always shadowed. They may hold ancient water ice delivered by comets and asteroids.

★ Caloris Basin is Mercury's largest meteorite impact crater. It is 1,550 kilometers (960 miles) across.

★ Fast-orbiting Mercury was named for the Roman messenger god. He zipped around on winged sandals.

★ To see Mercury, look for a dim planet close to the horizon in the western sky during the hour after sunset. Or look for it in the eastern sky during the hour before sunrise.

Mission Fast Facts

★ No astronauts have been to Mercury. Only robotic space probes have visited.

★ Mercury is a difficult planet for spacecraft to visit. The nearby Sun's heat and dangerous rays can damage spacecraft.

★ *Mariner 10* was the first spacecraft sent to the planet Mercury. It was the only one for more than 30 years. *Mariner 10* flew by Mercury in 1974–1975.

★ *Mariner 10* measured temperatures on Mercury and its magnetic field and looked for an atmosphere. It photographed about half of Mercury's surface, finding a crater- and cliff-covered world.

FAST FACTS ABOUT MERCURY

★

★ *MErcury Surface, Space ENvironment, GEochemistry, and Ranging (MESSENGER)* launched in 2004.

★ *MESSENGER* is a robotic orbiter spacecraft. It will make three flybys before going into orbit of Mercury in 2011.

★ *MESSENGER* will map nearly the entire planet in color. It will also measure Mercury's surface materials, its exosphere, and its magnetic field.

★ Both *Mariner 10* and *MESSENGER* used Venus's gravity to slingshot toward Mercury without getting pulled in by the Sun. This is called a gravity assist.

Mercury Timeline
of Exploration and Discovery

(Years given for missions are when spacecraft explored Mercury. These explorations happened years after launch.)

PREHISTORY Ancient peoples watch this shining object speed across the night sky.

265 B.C. Greek scientists study Mercury in the morning and evening skies.

1610 Galileo Galilei observes Mercury through a telescope.

1631 Pierre Gassendi uses a telescope to watch Mercury transit the Sun.

1639 Giovanni Zupus discovers that Mercury has phases, like Earth's moon.

1889 Giovanni Schiaparelli draws maps of Mercury's surface.

circa 1900 Astronomers incorrectly declare that Mercury spins once per orbit.

1965 Astronomers use radar to discover that Mercury spins three times for every two orbits.

1968 Moon probe *Surveyor 7* takes pictures of Mercury from the Moon.

1974–1975 Space probe *Mariner 10* becomes the first spacecraft to fly by Mercury, photographing about half of Mercury's surface in three passes.

1991 Radar astronomers on Earth detect possible evidence for water ice deep inside shadowed craters near Mercury's poles.

2008–2009 *MErcury Surface, Space ENvironment, GEochemistry, and Ranging* (*MESSENGER*) space probe flies by three times, discovering volcanoes and giant craters on the never-before-seen side of Mercury.

2011 *MESSENGER* to begin year-long polar orbit of Mercury.

2020 BepiColombo's two orbiters to map Mercury and investigate its magnetosphere after a 2014 launch.

THIS illustration shows *MESSENGER* arriving at Mercury in 2008.

CHAPTER 2

MESSENGER TO MERCURY

Waiting for a robotic spacecraft to get where it is going is stressful. On January 14, 2008, scientists paced around a conference room filled with computers. A glass wall separated them from busy mission control. *MESSENGER* was closing in on Mercury. There was nothing for the scientists to do but wait. "The *MESSENGER* Science Team is extremely excited about this flyby," Sean Solomon told reporters. "We are about to enjoy our first close-up view of Mercury in more than three decades." Sean Solomon is the scientist in charge of the *MESSENGER* mission.

IN 2008, *MESSENGER* photographed this never-before-seen side of Mercury. Notice the number of giant craters with bright rays.

WORTH THE TRIP

The name *MESSENGER* stands for *MErcury Surface, Space ENvironment, GEochemistry, and Ranging.* The space probe was launched in the summer of 2004. Three and half years later, *MESSENGER* made its first pass by Mercury. Everyone clapped in the conference room as the first of 1,200 images lit up computer screens. Many of the pictures showed parts of Mercury that had never been seen before. "[I]t's like being a tourist in a place that no one has gone," Solomon told reporters.

Engineers had to build a new kind of spacecraft to get to Mercury. But *MESSENGER* flew by the smallest planet like a pro. In October of 2008, *MESSENGER* made its second pass. The spacecraft flew just 201 kilometers (125 miles) above Mercury's cratered surface. It mapped a South America-sized chunk of Mercury never seen before. "When combined with data from our first flyby and from *Mariner 10,* our latest coverage means that we have now seen about 95 percent of the planet," Solomon said. Making a map of all of Mercury is a big part of *MESSENGER*'s mission. But scientists want more than a better view. They want answers to all kind of questions about Mercury.

FAR-OUT FACT

SURVIVING THE SUN

A sunshade protects *MESSENGER* from the Sun's heat and damaging rays. The sunshade can keep the spacecraft's electronics and instruments at room temperature even when it's heated to 370° Celsius (about 700° Fahrenheit). *MESSENGER* will fly 7.9 billion kilometers (4.9 billion miles) on its way to Mercury. It will eventually circle the Sun a dozen times. With each loop *MESSENGER* will get a bit closer to Mercury without falling into the Sun.

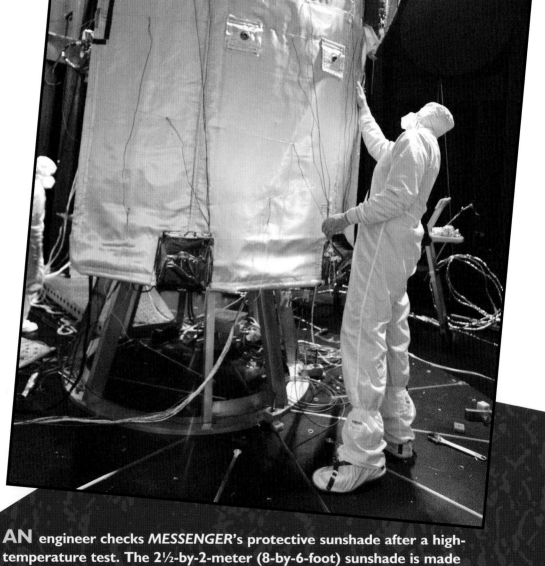

AN engineer checks *MESSENGER*'s protective sunshade after a high-temperature test. The 2½-by-2-meter (8-by-6-foot) sunshade is made of a special ceramic fabric.

EARTH'S BROTHER

Why study Mercury? Because it is a terrestrial planet, like Earth, Venus, and Mars. "We have four siblings that all had a similar birthing process four and a half billion years ago. Of course, we live on one of them," Sean Solomon explained. If we want to take care of Earth, we need "to understand how our planet works, how it came to be." Learning Mercury's history and how it formed can teach us about our own planet.

SHRINKING PLANET, GIANT VOLCANOES

One question *MESSENGER* is working on is: Why is the smallest planet getting even smaller? Mercury used to be about four kilometers (2.5 miles) or so wider than it is today. The planet's center, or core, is what's shrinking. Mercury has a giant melted iron core. *MESSENGER* measured Mercury's core. It's now about 60 percent of the planet's mass. The core's metal has cooled and shrunk over the past 3.8 billion years. *MESSENGER* found that the amount the core has shrunk ". . . is at least one third greater than we previously thought," said Sean Solomon.

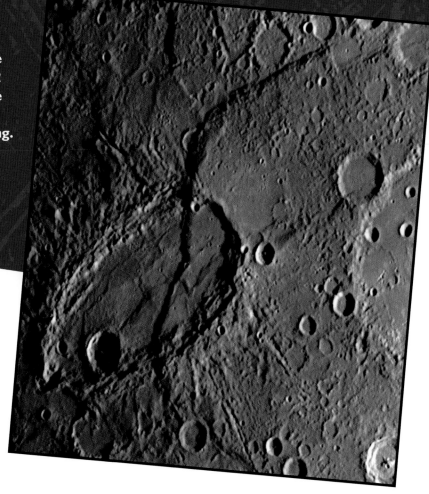

The shrinking caused Mercury's surface to wrinkle up like a raisin. The surface scrunched up into long steep cliffs, called rupes. "They tell us how important the cooling core has been to the evolution of the surface," explained Solomon.

Mercury's volcanoes are another mystery *MESSENGER* is solving. Its two cameras are sending back detailed pictures of the planet's surface. Many more volcanoes than expected are showing up in the new close-up images—some as big as Delaware! Mercury's volcanoes are ancient. They stopped spewing lava billions of years ago. Scientists wondered what created Mercury's smooth plains. Thanks to *MESSENGER* they now know that floods of lava created them.

Like many space missions, *MESSENGER* is creating new questions, too. It found mysterious bluish material all over Mercury. It might have come out of the planet's core as lava long ago. But scientists do not know yet what the mysterious stuff is.

FAR-OUT FACT

WHAT'S IT CALLED?

MESSENGER is discovering new craters, volcanoes, rupes, and other fascinating features. In 2008, the *MESSENGER* team named twelve features on Mercury's surface. They include ten new craters named for artists and writers. Cliffs or rupes are named for the ships of famous explorers. Beagle Rupes is named for the ship of naturalist Charles Darwin. And Pantheon Fossae, an area of hundreds of narrow trenches (called fossae), is named for the Pantheon temple of ancient Rome.

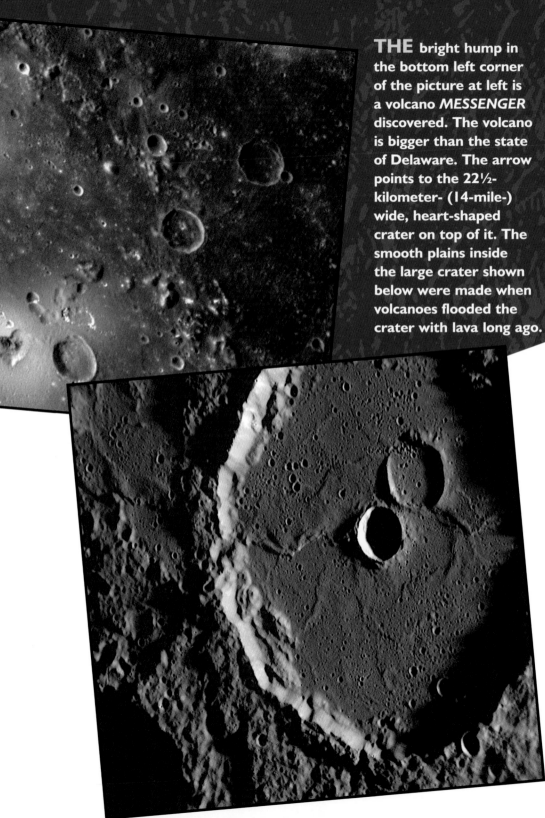

THE bright hump in the bottom left corner of the picture at left is a volcano *MESSENGER* discovered. The volcano is bigger than the state of Delaware. The arrow points to the 22½-kilometer- (14-mile-) wide, heart-shaped crater on top of it. The smooth plains inside the large crater shown below were made when volcanoes flooded the crater with lava long ago.

ICY EXOSPHERE?

Mercury has no atmosphere, but it has an exosphere. "An exosphere is the upper part of any planetary atmosphere," explained Sean Solomon. It is where just a few scattered atoms of air remain. "But Mercury is entirely exosphere . . . all the way down to the surface." The Sun gives off a constant stream of charged particles, called the solar wind. The solar wind creates Mercury's exosphere. The wind blows bits of Mercury's surface off into space.

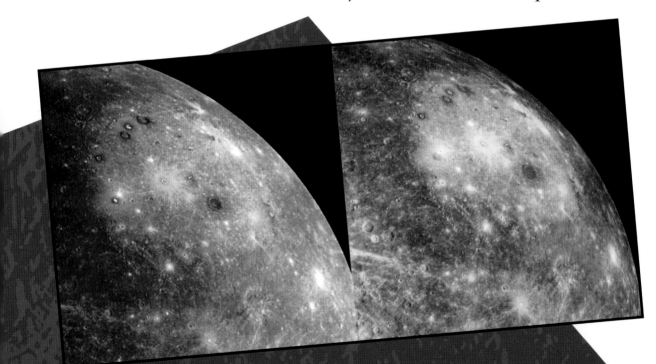

CALORIS Basin is Mercury's biggest crater. It is so big that Texas could fit inside it! The left picture shows Caloris Basin in true color. The right picture has added colors to highlight the different minerals that make up Mercury's surface.

Studying what is in Mercury's exosphere can tell scientists what makes up its surface.

MESSENGER is equipped with an exosphere-studying instrument. When it started sending back findings, scientists were surprised. Besides calcium and sodium in the exosphere, *MESSENGER* found water. Could it be coming

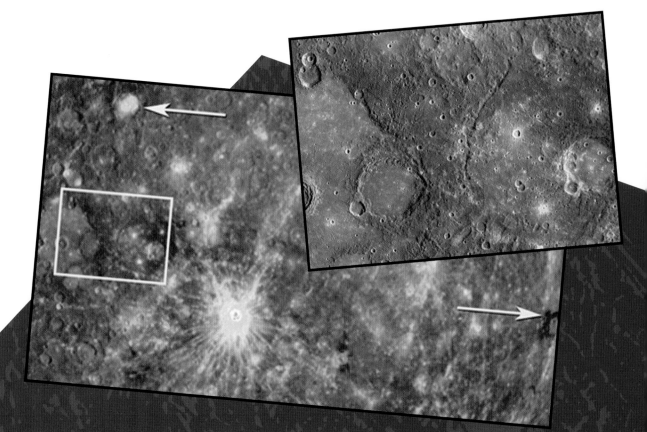

SCIENTISTS added color to this *MESSENGER* image. The colors highlight the different materials on Mercury's surface. The light blue lines are rays from young impact craters. The arrow on the left points to bright material most likely from a volcanic eruption long ago. The right arrow points to one of the areas of mysterious dark bluish material on Mercury. You can see the area in the white box closer up in the smaller picture, top right.

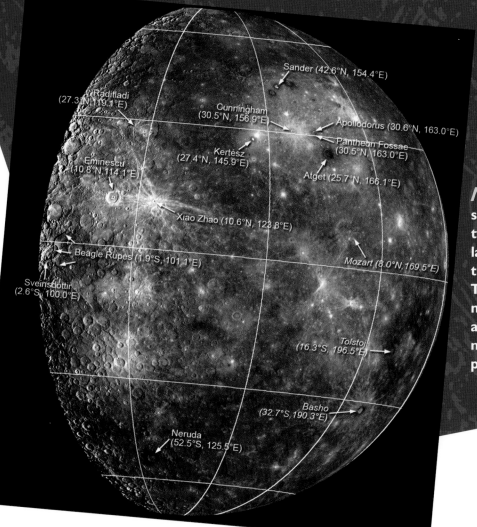

Sander (42.6°N, 154.4°E)

Raditladi (27.3°N, 119.1°E)

Cunningham (30.5°N, 156.9°E)

Apollodorus (30.6°N, 163.0°E)

Pantheon Fossae (30.5°N, 163.0°E)

Kertész (27.4°N, 145.9°E)

Eminescu (10.8°N, 114.1°E)

Atget (25.7°N, 166.1°E)

Xiao Zhao (10.6°N, 123.8°E)

Beagle Rupes (1.9°S, 101.1°E)

Mozart (8.0°N, 169.5°E)

Sveinsdóttir (2.6°S, 100.0°E)

Tolstoj (16.3°S, 196.5°E)

Basho (32.7°S, 190.3°E)

Neruda (52.5°S, 125.5°E)

MESSENGER scientists identified twelve of the fifteen landforms labeled on this map of Mercury. The three craters named Basho, Tolstoj, and Mozart were named from *Mariner 10* photographs.

from icy craters at Mercury's poles? The dark shadowed ones that radar telescopes saw ice in? Maybe. A closer look at the poles will provide more clues. But that will have to wait. "[S]ome of the observations we are most eager to make . . . will not be possible until *MESSENGER* begins to orbit the innermost planet," said Sean Solomon.

CHAPTER 3

WHAT'S NEXT FOR MERCURY?

The pictures and information sent by the *MESSENGER* space probe have already changed Mercury's image. The planet is no longer seen as a dead hunk of hot rock. Mercury is instead a constantly changing world. It is a terrestrial planet like Earth, Venus, and Mars, with its own unique history.

More of Mercury's mysteries will likely be solved by *MESSENGER* in the future. The spacecraft will begin studying the smallest planet in depth in 2011. *MESSENGER* will become an orbiter. It will circle Mercury for at least one Earth year. The orbiter will

BEPICOLOMBO will be made up of four parts. The parts will separate once the spacecraft reaches Mercury. This illustration shows them from left to right: The solar-powered vehicle that carries it all to Mercury, the *Mercury Planetary Orbiter*, a protective sunshield, and the *Mercury Magnetospheric Orbiter*.

FAR-OUT FACT

IN HONOR OF BEPI

The BepiColombo mission is named for Giuseppe (Bepi) Colombo (1920–1984). He was an Italian mathematician and engineer. Colombo studied how planets and suns orbit and spin. He also gave advice to space agencies planning missions, including the first to Mercury, *Mariner 10*. It was his idea to send *Mariner 10* into a solar orbit. The solar orbit allowed it to fly by Mercury three times, instead of just once. Colombo's idea is what made *Mariner 10* such a success.

AN INTERNATIONAL MISSION

Studying Mercury is an international effort by many countries. *MESSENGER* is a mission of the American space agency, NASA. BepiColombo is a cooperative mission between the European Space Agency (ESA) and JAXA, the Japanese space agency. ESA is building the *Mercury Planetary Orbiter* in Germany, Italy, France, and the United Kingdom. JAXA is building the *Mercury Magnetospheric Orbiter* in Japan. A Russian rocket will launch the spacecraft from the South American country of French Guiana.

track Mercury's changing exosphere and magnetic field. *MESSENGER* will go around the planet from pole to pole. This will give it a good view of those always-dark craters at Mercury's north and south poles. Do you think *MESSENGER* will find ice in them?

CIRCLING IN ON MERCURY

Not long after *MESSENGER's* mission ends, another spacecraft is scheduled to head to Mercury.

THIS illustration shows a closer orbit path (in red) for the *Mercury Planetary Orbiter*. *Mercury Magnetospheric Orbiter* circles farther out along a yellow path to study Mercury's magnetosphere.

★

BepiColombo is a mission to send two orbiters to Mercury. The two spacecraft will launch as one around 2014. They will travel to Mercury for six years. Once at the planet, they will break apart into separate space probes (as illustrated on pages 38–39). Each will orbit Mercury for about a year.

The *Mercury Planetary Orbiter* will loop closely around the planet. Its cameras and instruments will map Mercury. It will study the planet's surface and inside structure. The *Mercury Magnetospheric Orbiter* will orbit farther away from the planet. It will study Mercury's magnetosphere. This is the area around the planet affected by its magnetic field. Mercury is the only other terrestrial planet besides Earth with a significant magnetic field. Scientists do not know yet how such a small planet creates a magnetic field. It is one of Mercury's many remaining mysteries.

Words to Know

asteroid—A large rock that orbits the Sun.

astronomer—A scientist who studies what is in space, such as moons, stars, and planets.

atmosphere—The gases that surround a planet, moon, or other object in space.

comet—A large chunk of frozen gases, ice, and dust that orbits the Sun.

core—The center of a planet, moon, or star.

craters—Bowl-shaped holes made by impact explosions, often from comet or asteroid crashes.

day—The time it takes an object in space to complete one turn or spin.

exosphere—The outermost region of an atmosphere where atoms are scarce.

flyby probe—A space probe that flies by a planet or moon.

fossae—Narrow troughs or trenches.

geochemistry—The study of the kinds of chemicals in rocks and minerals.

gravity—The force of attraction between two or more bodies that have mass.

instrument—A scientific tool or device.

lava—Melted rock that comes out of a volcano.

magnetic field—The area of magnetic influence around a magnet, electric current, or planet.

WORDS TO KNOW

★

magnetosphere—The region of space influenced by the magnetic field of a planet or moon.

mass—The amount of matter in something.

meteor—A rock from space that is traveling through an atmosphere; a shooting star.

observatory—A place with telescopes and other instruments for observing planets, stars, and other objects in space.

orbit—The circling path followed by a planet, moon, or other object in space around another object; to move around an object in space.

orbiter—A space probe that orbits a planet, moon, or other object in space.

radar—A technology or device that uses reflected radio waves to find or map distant or unseen objects.

ranging—Finding the distances between objects to map landscapes.

rupes—Long cliffs on Mercury's surface.

solar system—A sun and everything that orbits it.

solar wind—The constant stream of charged particles given off by the Sun.

space probe—A robotic spacecraft launched into space to collect information.

terrestrial planet—A rocky solid planet with a metal core, including Mercury, Venus, Earth, and Mars.

volcano—A break in a planet's or moon's surface where melted rock or gas escape.

water vapor—Water in gas form.

Find Out More and Get Updates

BOOKS

Bourgeois, Paulette. *The Jumbo Book of Space.* Toronto: Kids Can Press, 2007.

Carson, Mary Kay. *Exploring the Solar System: A History with 22 Activities.* Chicago: Chicago Review Press, 2008.

Elkins-Tanton, Linda T. *The Sun, Mercury and Venus.* New York: Facts on File, 2006.

Fraknoi, Andrew. *Disney's Wonderful World of Space.* New York: Disney Publishing, 2007.

Miller, Ron. *Mercury and Pluto.* Brookfield, Conn.: Twenty-First Century Books, 2003.

FIND OUT MORE AND GET UPDATES
★

MERCURY EXPLORATIONS WEB SITE

Johns Hopkins University Applied Physics Lab. "*MESSENGER* for Students." 1999–2009.
<http://btc.montana.edu/messenger/students/student_index.php>

MERCURY MOVIES

Johns Hopkins University Applied Physics Lab. "*MESSENGER* Movies." 1999–2009.
<http://messenger.jhuapl.edu/the_mission/movies.html>

PLANET-WATCHING WEB SITES

Space.com. "NightSky Sky Calendar."
<http://www.space.com/spacewatch/sky_calendar.html>

The University of Texas McDonald Observatory. "StarDate: Planet Viewing." 1995–2009.
<http://stardate.org/nightsky/planets>

SOLAR SYSTEM WEB SITES

NASA. "Solar System Exploration: Kids." July 2008.
<http://solarsystem.nasa.gov/kids>

Randy Russell. "Windows to the Universe: Mercury." June 2009.
<http://www.windows.ucar.edu>
Click on "Our Solar System." Then click on "Mercury."

47

Index